For the glory of Old State,
For her founders strong and great,

For the future that we wait,
Raise the song, raise the song.

Sing our love and loyalty,
Sing our hopes that bright and free

Rest, O Mother dear, with thee,
All with thee, all with thee.

When we stood at childhood's gate,
Shapeless in the hands of fate,

Thou didst mold us, dear old State,
Dear old State, dear old State.

May no act of ours bring shame,
To one heart that loves thy name,

May our lives but swell thy fame,
Dear old State, dear old State.

— Fred Lewis Pattee

The Pennsylvania State University

GIFT OF THE CLASS OF

OLD MAIN

Raise the Song

The Pennsylvania State University

Photography by

Dan Beigel

Harmony House Publishers

Published by Harmony House Publishers - Louisville
P. O. Box 90 Prospect, Kentucky 40059
502-228-2010

First Edition Printed in China 2003

Photography © Dan Beigel
Additional campus photographs courtesy Penn State University Publications
and Penn State Athletics
Archival Photography - The Pennsylvania State University
Executive Editor: William Strode
Layout and Design: Boz Johnson

Library of Congress Number: 2002106943
Hardcover ISBN: 1-56469-099-7

GEORGE W. ATHERTON, LL.D.
JUNE 20, 1837 – JULY 24, 1906.
CAPTAIN CO. G, 10 REGT.
CONN. VOLS. 1861 — 63.
PRESIDENT
THE PENNSYLVANIA
STATE COLLEGE
1882 — 1906

For the glory of Old State,
For her founders strong and great,

For the future that we wait,
Raise the song, raise the song.

Sing our love and loyalty,
Sing our hopes that bright and free

Rest, O Mother dear, with thee,
All with thee, all with thee.

When we stood at childhood's gate,
Shapeless in the hands of fate,

Thou didst mold us, dear old State,
Dear old State, dear old State.

May no act of ours bring shame,
To one heart that loves thy name,

May our lives but swell thy fame,
Dear old State, dear old State.

Pillsbury

s, 3 x p

Foreword

Since its founding in 1855, Penn State has served Pennsylvania and the nation through its rich history of teaching, research, and service, earning a reputation as one of the best public universities in the world.

I am gratified by the contributions Penn State makes each day to human development, economic development, and cultural development, while offering students an incredibly enriching academic experience. Penn State is the birthplace of ideas and a home for wondrous discovery. Our students and faculty have earned many honors along the way, and our research has led to some of the greatest advances of our time, from the sighting of the first atom to the discovery of the first planets outside our solar system to the development of life-saving medical devices.

Our alumni have gone on to lead Fortune 500 companies, serve as governors and cabinet officers, earn the Nobel Prize, win Academy Awards, command troops, create magnificent works of art, author best-selling novels, and direct humanitarian efforts across the world — all the while adding prestige and honor to the Penn State name.

Within the pages of this book you will find a brief view of the history of Penn State, a current look at its many facets, and a celebration of its promising future. No publication can fully capture the legacy of our great University, but *Raise the Song* provides a unique collection of photographs and vignettes that paint a colorful portrait of a dynamic university pursuing excellence at every turn. *Raise the Song* will evoke fond memories and a deep sense of pride in anyone who is a Nittany Lion.

That pride is well-founded.

With its 24 campus locations, Penn State is a vital collection of learning communities reaching every corner of the Commonwealth, touching nearly every citizen in some way. Today, one in every two Pennsylvania households has at least one person participating in a Penn State program. Throughout its impressive history, the University has conferred more than 565,000 degrees.

As you look through this wonderful chronology of memories and achievements, you will see that Penn State's extraordinary success is clearly a product of its people and the established strengths and traditions that were carefully nurtured throughout the University's history. It is on this firm foundation that we will continue to build, setting new standards of excellence, seeking new discoveries, and educating new generations.

I hope you share my pride in all that has been achieved at Penn State and my enthusiasm for all that will be accomplished in the years to come. Let us do as the Alma Mater suggests and "Raise the Song" in praise of our wonderful University.

Graham B. Spanier
President, The Pennsylvania State University

DuBois Campus

New Kensington Campus

Wilkes-Barre Campus

104
COLLEGE OF
THE LIBERAL ARTS
TRACEY MELNICK

WEATHER WORLD
EFF 2
WPSX 3
WPSX 3

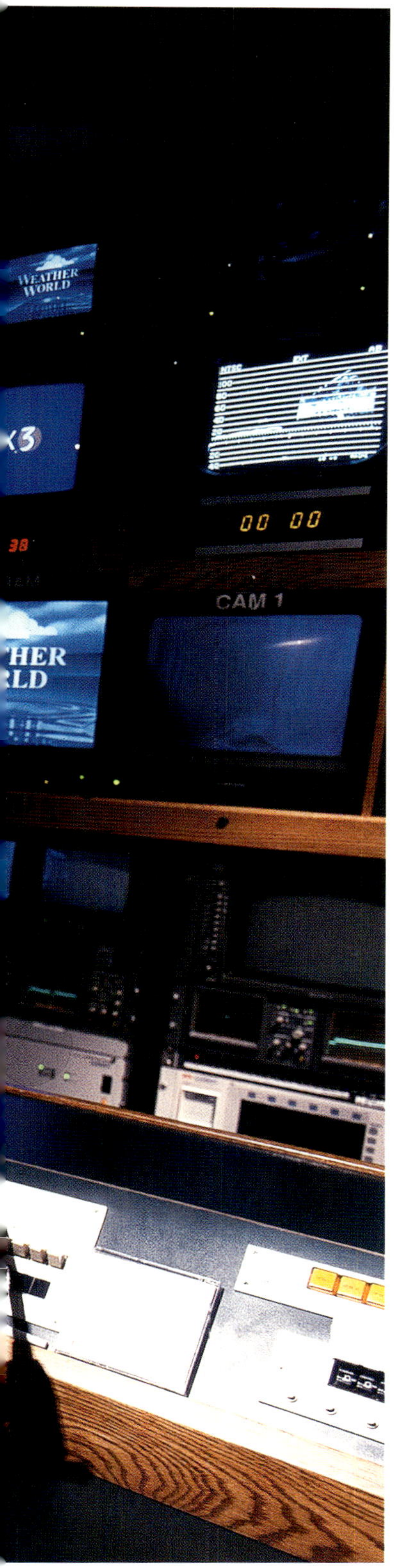
WEATHER WORLD
CAM 1

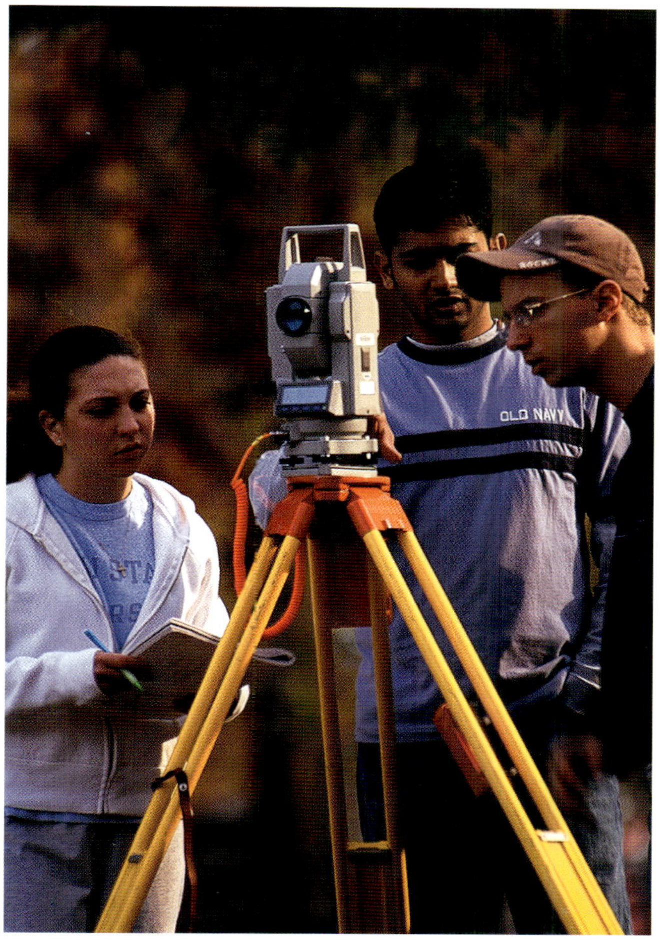
OLD NAVY

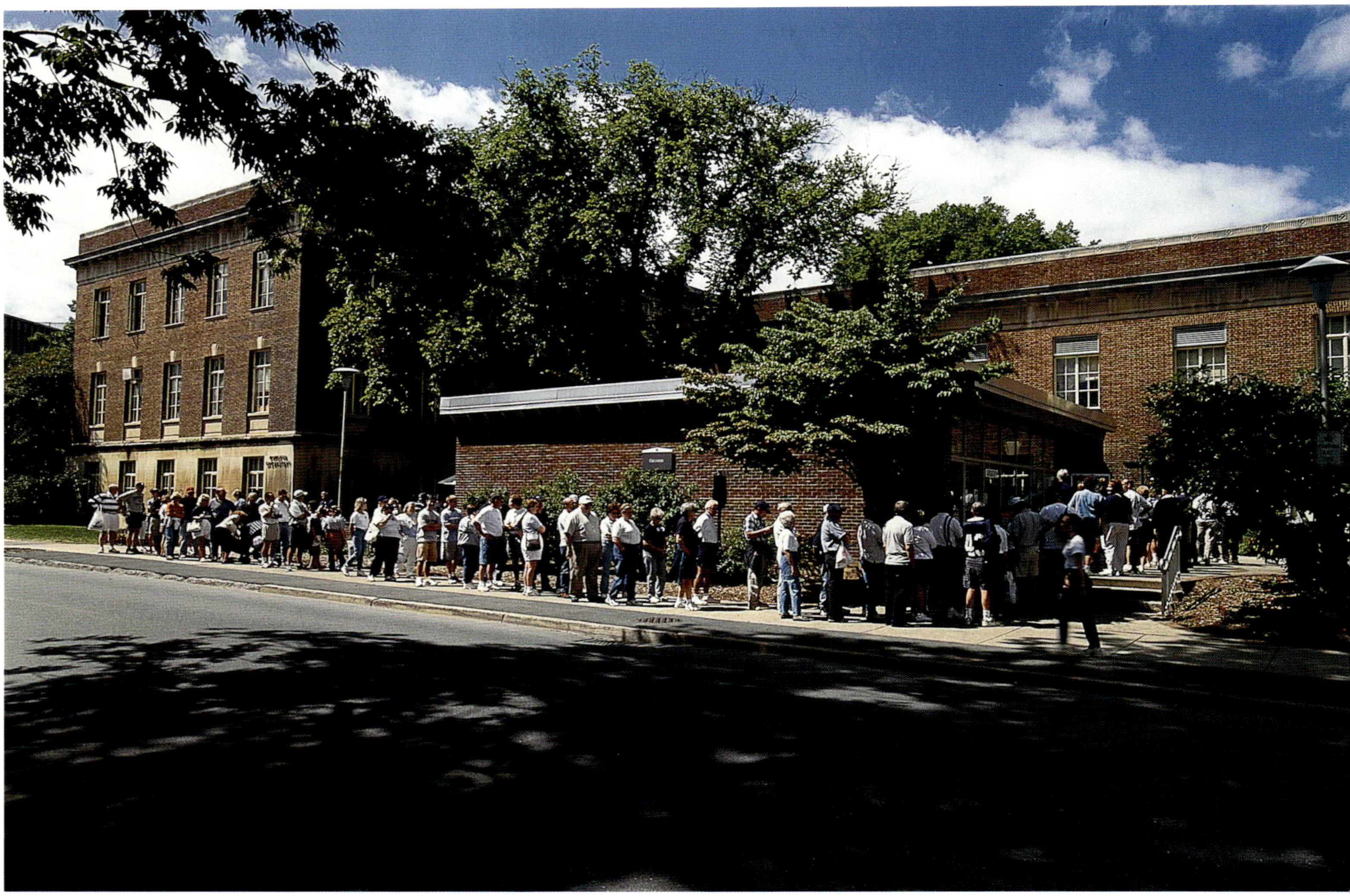

WE ARE
PENN STATE

ALLEN STREET GRILL
The CORNER
The CORNE

BUD BUD BUD

S. Allen St.

THE PATERNO LEGACY

Friendship

START

GOOD GRIEF, CHARLIE BROWN
SWE
TRIANGLE
CELEBRATE OLD STATE

ΣΦΝ

PennState

Good fans are hard to come by
Celebrate Safety
TOYOTA
PEPSI
13
PENN STATE ATHLETICS

6466
Reduced Fat
Wheat Thins
Corona
RIPPLES

NIKE

PennState
PNC
PENN STATE 7 0:41 USM 7
DOWN 3RD TO GO 7 BALL ON 12 QTR 1
TOYOTA
PEPSI
GoPSUsports.com
Go Lions!

PennState
O
P
S
U

SJ

PENN STATE
BLUE BAND
ALUMNI

50

30

PennState
PNC
PEPSI
Let's go
BOO GONK
Neotech

BOO GONK

PENN STATE
23

PENN STATE
33
PENN STATE
3

PENN STATE
PENN STATE

1819
1821

SAINT FRANCIS
PENN STATE
1969
PENN STATE
1931
PENN STATE
1934
PENN STATE
1940
GUELPH
1833
1922
1991
GW
1822

PENN STATE
8
PENN STATE
15

15
10
Penn State
19
Penn

622

PENN STATE
6
PENN STATE
8

PennState
PENN STATE
PENN STATE

GREGG ELECTRONICS
RAMA

For Her Founders

For the glory of Old State,
For her founders strong and great,

For the future that we wait,
Raise the song, raise the song.

Sing our love and loyalty,
Sing our hopes that bright and free

Rest, O Mother dear, with thee,
All with thee, all with thee.

When we stood at childhood's gate,
Shapeless in the hands of fate,

Thou didst mold us, dear old State,
Dear old State, dear old State.

May no act of ours bring shame,
To one heart that loves thy name,

May our lives but swell thy fame,
Dear old State, dear old State.

Evan Pugh

For Her Founders, Strong and Great

On July 2, 1862, President Abraham Lincoln signed into law the Morrill Land-Grant Act, which provided federal support for a new kind of higher education. The national system of land-grant colleges and universities established under the act pledged to offer a broad program of studies in agriculture, engineering, the applied sciences, and other subjects having practical value, as well as studies in the liberal arts and sciences. The Pennsylvania legislature in 1863 designated the institution that would one day become The Pennsylvania State University as the Commonwealth's sole land-grant institution.

But the concept of land-grant education was so novel that few college leaders at first fully grasped its significance. That was true at Penn State, following the death of its visionary first president, Evan Pugh, in 1864. In addition, the Commonwealth provided meager financial support, and the complex procedure of federal funding likewise produced little income. Consequently, Penn State drifted, not making its academic mark in any particular way and in danger of closing its doors, until George W. Atherton assumed the presidency in 1882. Atherton clearly understood the meaning of the land-grant mission of teaching, research, and public service. Under his leadership, Penn State was reborn. It expanded its course offerings in many fields in response to the growing and diverse needs of the state and nation it served. It also initiated its first systematic research and outreach programs.

From those sometimes uncertain nineteenth century beginnings has emerged one of America's largest and most distinguished public universities. The photographs and timeline that follow afford a glimpse of that rise to greatness.

Primitive by later standards, this chemistry lab in Old Main epitomized state-of-the-art instruction in the 1870s.

A horse-drawn lawn mower maintains the grounds around Old Main, circa 1880.

1855

Governor James Pollock signs the charter incorporating The Farmers' High School.

James Irvin gives 200 acres to locate the school in Centre County.

1861

Eleven students receive baccalaureate degrees at the first commencement.

1863

The Pennsylvania legislature designates the Agricultural College the Commonwealth's sole land-grant institution.

Old Main is completed.

The college awards its first graduate degrees (two master's degrees in agriculture).

1851

The Pennsylvania State Agricultural Society is formed in Harrisburg.

1859

Dr. Evan Pugh, an agricultural chemist, is named first president.

The first class of 69 students is enrolled.

1862

President Abraham Lincoln signs the Morrill Act, leading to the establishment of a national system of land-grant colleges.

The Farmers' High School changes its name to the Agricultural College of Pennsylvania.

1864

Evan Pugh dies, and an 18-year period of weak leadership and curricular drift begins.

College Avenue, visible in the center of this early 1890s photo, then as now defined the boundary between town and campus.

George W. Atherton

President Atherton, front row at right, with the Penn State faculty, 1887.

1870

The Penn State Alumni Association is organized.

1871

President James Calder eliminates tuition.

1879

A state commission alleges the college is "very badly managed" and has failed to win the confidence of the citizenry.

1882

George W. Atherton, a nationally renowned proponent of land-grant education, is named president.

1883

Courses of study are expanded to include engineering, science, agriculture, and the liberal arts.

1887

The state legislature begins making biennial (later annual) financial appropriations to the college.

Penn State plays its first intercollegiate football game under modern rules, defeating Bucknell 54-0. Pink and black are selected as the team colors

The Freelance, earliest predecessor of the Daily Collegian, begins publication.

1888

The Agricultural Experiment Station is founded to promote a more scientific approach to research.

The first two fraternities are founded: chapters of Phi Gamma Delta and Beta Theta Pi.

1889

First publication of LaVie, the college yearbook.

Old Botany Building with its formal gardens and greenhouse, as seen from the bell tower of Old Main in the mid-1890s.

Construction of Schwab Auditorium is nearing completion in this 1903 scene.

Professor Fred Pattee, center, conducts a class in "bibliography" in the college library in Old Main.

1890

Students adopt dark blue and white as the college's official colors.

The first international student earns a baccalaureate degree, Potter M. Brown of New Zealand.

1892

Correspondence courses (in agriculture) are initiated, among the first formal outreach programs in the nation.

Penn State introduces the nation's first collegiate instruction in ice cream making.

1896

State College Borough is incorporated with about 300 residents.

1900

The Cadet band, predecessor of the Blue Band, is formed.

Undergraduate enrollment reaches a record 281 students.

1901

Fred Pattee writes the Alma Mater.

1902

James G. White '82 makes a gift to endow the first scholarship fund.

1903

Schwab Auditorium is completed, a gift from steel magnate Charles Schwab.

1904

Carnegie Library opens, a gift from Andrew Carnegie.

H. D. "Joe" Mason '07 "invents" the Nittany Lion mascot at a baseball game against Princeton.

This 1914 view of Old Main shows the bell tower and roofline that replaced the originals following a minor fire in 1892.

Playing baseball on Old Beaver Field. Part of Frear Lab would later occupy the site of the grandstand.

Penn State and the University of Pennsylvania were fierce gridiron rivals in the early 1900s.

1905

Calvin H. Waller earns a bachelor's degree in agriculture, becoming Penn State's first African-American graduate.

1906

President Atherton dies.

1907

The Student Board, the first official student government organization, is created.

1908

Incoming president Edwin E. Sparks vows to "take the college to the people" via extension programs.

Enrollment surpasses 1,000.

1910

First formal summer session, a continuing education program attended by 146 school teachers.

1911

Penn State-in-China program is organized to sustain international agricultural research and teaching.

1912

An engineering "branch school" in Allentown becomes Penn State's first permanent off-campus instructional location.

The School of Agriculture helps to implement the county agent system, roots of Penn State Cooperative Extension.

1915

Infirmary opens in Ihlseng Cottage, soon comes under the supervision of Dr Joseph P. Ritenour.

In this World War I publicity pose, President Sparks shucks corn, doing his part to encourage food production.

In the 1930s, women's athletics consisted of instruction in physical education—such as this class in badminton—and intramurals.

The old Dairy Barn, near the intersection of Curtin and Shortlidge Roads, was a campus landmark that lasted well into the 1960s.

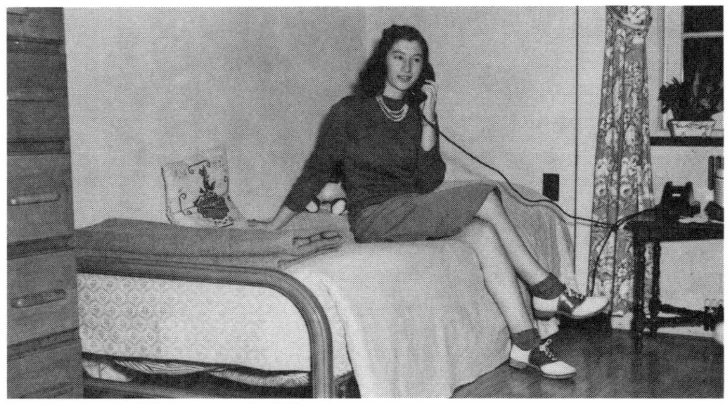

Room telephones were a luxury when Atherton Hall opened in 1938.

1916

Congress establishes the Reserve Officers Training Corps (ROTC), although Penn State had been offering military instruction since the Civil War.

1920

State Chamber of Commerce survey shows Penn State turning away 500 qualified applicants yearly for lack of space.

1921

Trustees approve emergency Building Fund campaign under President John M. Thomas to raise $2 million in private gifts for new facilities.

First broadcast of college-owned radio station WPAB (later changed to WPSC).

1923

Nittany Lions make first appearance in the Rose Bowl.

1926

First Ph.D. awarded, to Marsh W. White in physics.

First national sorority (Chi Omega) establishes a Penn State chapter.

Ralph D. Hetzel becomes Penn State's ninth president.

1927

Using a combination of state and private funds, a construction boom begins that will result in a new Old Main, the Nittany Lion Inn and Rec Hall, among other landmark structures.

1929

Mont Alto state forestry school merges with Penn State.

1934

Undergraduate centers opened in Hazleton, Pottsville, Uniontown and Sayre-Towanda.

1935

DuBois replaces the Sayre-Towanda Center.

A physics experiment in Osmond Lab, about 1930.

Ralph D. Hetzel

Curtis-Wright Cadettes were non-degree students who received specialized wartime training for service in defense-related industries.

1937

Intercollegiate teams fielded in 14 sports (all men).

1938

4,500 acres in Stone Valley acquired for research, practicums, and recreation.

1940

Enrollment hits record of 6,514.

1945

Ordnance Research Laboratory (later Applied Research Lab) established, paving way for defense-related research.

1948

Nittany Lions break the color barrier at the Cotton Bowl by refusing to play without African-American teammates.

1950

Milton Eisenhower becomes president.

1952

50,000th degree conferred.

1953

The Pennsylvania State College becomes The Pennsylvania State University.

Dwight Eisenhower makes first of four visits to campus as U.S. President.

In 1940, cars could still be parked on campus along the Allen Street mall but the construction of Pattee Library had closed the route to through traffic.

Members of Penn State's Army Reserve Officers Training Corps unit, parading on College Avenue in 1940, were called to active duty soon thereafter.

Housing for married World War II veterans—the height of comfort for ex-G.I.'s accustomed to pup tents or ships' hammocks.

Penn State Altoona still occupied temporary quarters in the former Ivyside amusement park when this photo was taken in 1948.

The snack bar in Waring Hall was a prime site for informal socializing in the 1950s.

The card catalog room in Pattee Library—one of the campus's most important, if not exciting, locations.

College Avenue was still a two-way street in this view from about 1950.

On the eastern edge of campus, trailers in Windcrest and the Pollock Circle prefab units provided temporary housing for thousands of ex-G.I.'s who enrolled after World War II.

Upper classmen greet the "frosh" near Schwab Auditorium. The 1960s saw the almost total disappearance of freshman customs.

The "new" Old Main, circa 1950. Behind it is the Woman's Building, which later gave way to Oswald Tower.

East Halls is under construction in this 1960s view, when it was said to be the nation's largest campus residence hall complex.

Milton Eisenhower, and his brother, President of the United States Dwight Eisenhower, at Penn State's 1955 commencement.

1955

Breazeale Nuclear Reactor goes on-line.

1956

Eric Walker succeeds Milton Eisenhower as president.

1959

Commonwealth Campus system organized (Allentown, Altoona, Berks, DuBois, Erie, Hazleton, McKeesport, Mont Alto, New Kensington, Ogontz, Pottsville, Scranton, Wilkes-Barre and York).

1960

Beaver Stadium (moved from site on New Beaver Field) completed, capacity of 46,284.

1961

Study Abroad programs established.

1963

Milton S. Hershey Foundation and Trust gives Penn State $50 million to establish a medical center and college of medicine.

1965

First broadcast of University-owned-and-operated WPSX-TV.

1966

Penn State Harrisburg opens.

Residents of Packer Hall—part of the East Halls complex—pick up their mail circa 1967.

The Hetzel Union Building opened in 1954, was the campus's first permanent student union.

George Harrell, center, founding dean of the College of Medicine, shows a model of the Hershey Medical Center to President Eric Walker, right, and Penn State Trustee Roger Rowland.

1967

First class enrolled at the College of Medicine at The Milton S. Hershey Medical Center.

1969

Penn State ranks 12th nationally in total enrollment.

1970

John Oswald succeeds Eric Walker as president.

1973

Penn State Erie, the Behrend College, introduces four-year undergraduate programs.

1975

Alumni Vacation College initiated.

1982

Nittany Lions win first national championship in football.

1983

Bryce Jordan named president.

1987

Trustees approve 118-acre Research Park, later named Innovation Park, at Penn State.

Sign of the times: anti-Vietnam War rally in front of Old Main.

A less confrontational Old Main gathering: Gentle Thursday, an occasion to promote sharing and caring, was one of the most popular campus events of the 1970s.

Lunchtime in the Lion's Den, located in the HUB basement, in late 1960s.

Women's basketball helped to lead the way toward gender equity in intercollegiate athletics at Penn State.

Penn State Berks has occupied its current location since the Luersson Building (background) was completed in 1972.

A campus dining hall, about 1970.

West Halls remained a popular choice for student housing in the 1990s.

Learning at Penn State often means forging lifelong friendships.

President Bryce Jordan greets Bishop Desmond Tutu, one of the many distinguished visitors that Penn State hosts each year.

1989

Pennsylvania College of Technology affiliates with Penn State.

1990

Joab Thomas named president.

Big Ten Conference admits Penn State to membership.

1995

Graham Spanier named president.

1996

Schreyer Honors College endowed.

President Bill Clinton speaks at Graduate School commencement.

1997

Dickinson School of Law merges with Penn State.

1998

World Campus offers first courses.

2001

500,000th degree conferred.

2005

Penn State celebrates sesquicentennial.

Penn State is always building for the future.

For the glory of Old State,
For her founders strong and great,

For the future that we wait,
Raise the song, raise the song.

Sing our love and loyalty,
Sing our hopes that bright and free

Rest, O Mother dear, with thee,
All with thee, all with thee.

When we stood at childhood's gate,
Shapeless in the hands of fate,

Thou didst mold us, dear old State,
Dear old State, dear old State.

May no act of ours bring shame,
To one heart that loves thy name,

May our lives but swell thy fame,
Dear old State, dear old State.

PSU

ANTRIM

Altoona Campus

Hazleton Campus

Worthington Scranton Campus

Schuylkill Campus

Harrisburg Campus

Abington Campus

Shenango Campus

Erie Campus

Erie Campus

Fayette Campus

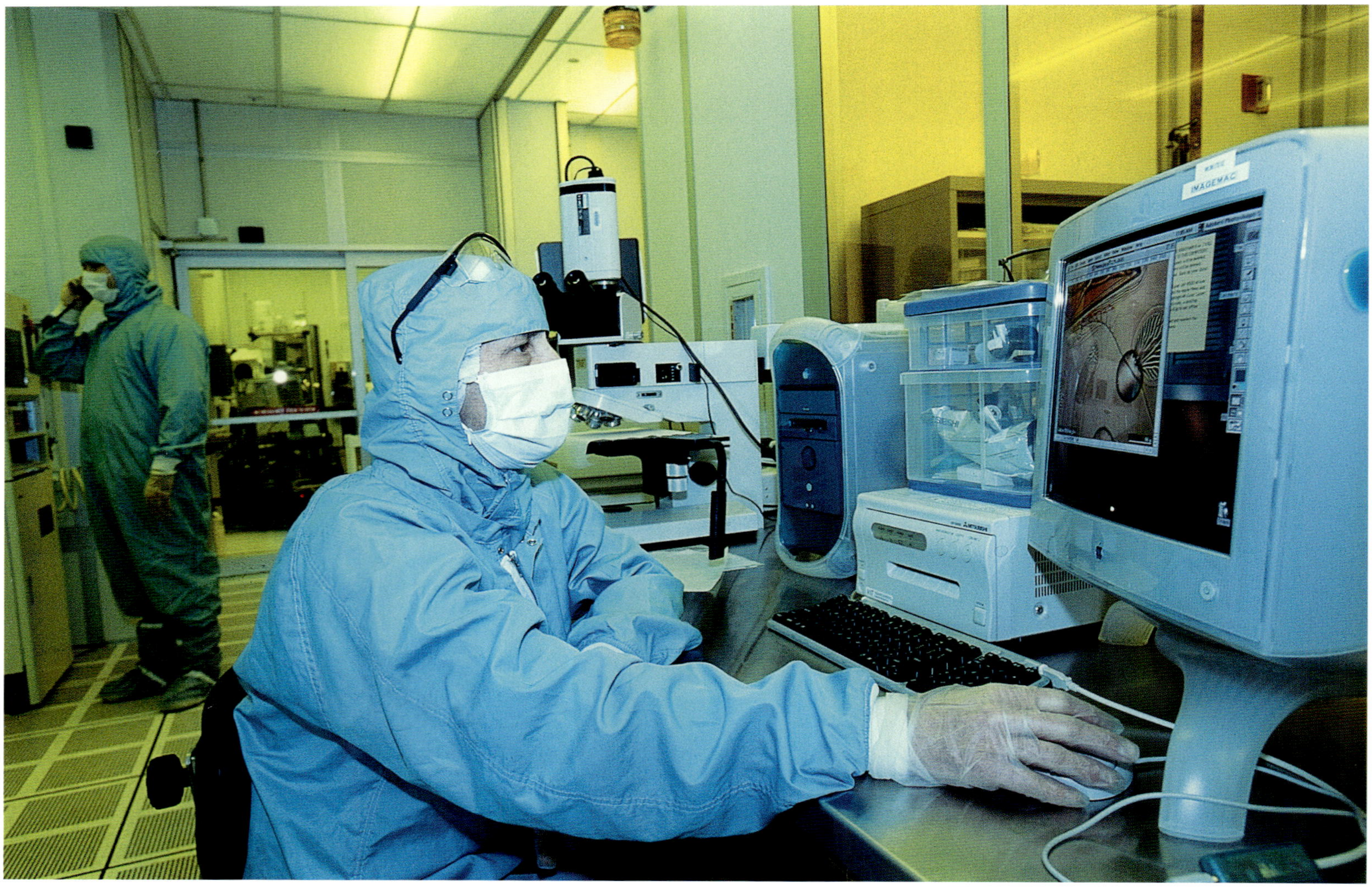
IMAGEMAC

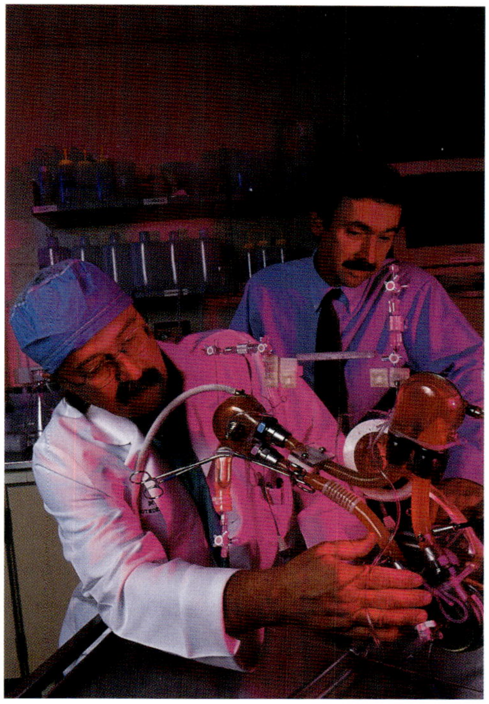

Mont Alto Campus

Penn College of Technology

Berks Campus

Berks Campus

Delaware County Campus

Hershey Medical Center

Worthington Scranton Campus

Lehigh Valley Campus

Beaver Campus

York Campus

Mont Alto Campus

McKeesport Campus

Great Valley Campus

The Dickinson School of Law

LIGHT AGE, INC.

World Campus

PENNSTATE
1855

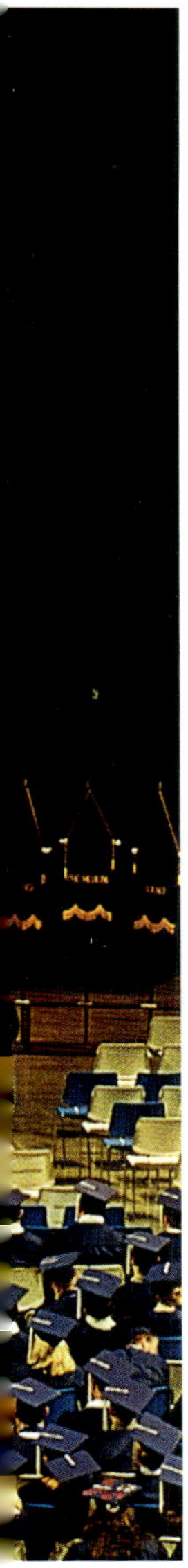